D0889724

OUR VAST HOME:
THE MILKY WAY AND OTHER GALAXIES

BY ISAAC ASIMOV
WITH REVISIONS AND UPDATING BY GREG WALZ-CHOJNACKI

Gareth Stevens Publishing
MILWAUKEE

For a free color catalog describing Gareth Stevens' list of high-quality books, call 1-800-542-2595 (USA) or 1-800-461-9120 (Canada). Gareth Stevens' Fax: (414) 225-0377.

Library of Congress Cataloging-in-Publication Data

Asimov, Isaac.
   Our vast home: the Milky Way and other galaxies / by Isaac Asimov; with
revisions and updating by Greg Walz-Chojnacki.
      p. cm. — (Isaac Asimov's New library of the universe)
   Rev. ed. of: Our Milky Way and other galaxies. 1988.
   Includes bibliographical references and index.
   ISBN 0-8368-1195-X
   1. Galaxies—Juvenile literature. 2. Milky Way—Juvenile literature.
[1. Galaxies. 2. Milky Way.] I. Walz-Chojnacki, Greg, 1954-. II. Asimov,
Isaac. Our Milky Way and other galaxies. III. Title. IV. Series: Asimov,
Isaac. New library of the universe.
QB857.3.A85   1995
523.1'12—dc20   94-32473

This edition first published in 1995 by
Gareth Stevens Publishing
1555 North RiverCenter Drive, Suite 201
Milwaukee, Wisconsin 53212, USA

Project editor: Barbara J. Behm
Design adaptation: Helene Feider
Editorial assistant: Diane Laska
Production director: Susan Ashley
Picture research: Kathy Keller
Artwork commissioning: Kathy Keller and Laurie Shock

Printed in the United States of America

1 2 3 4 5 6 7 8 9 99 98 97 96 95

To bring this classic of young people's information up to date, the editors at Gareth Stevens Publishing have selected two noted science authors, Greg Walz-Chojnacki and Francis Reddy. Walz-Chojnacki and Reddy coauthored the recent book *Celestial Delights: The Best Astronomical Events Through 2001.*

Walz-Chojnacki is also the author of the book *Comet: The Story Behind Halley's Comet* and various articles about the space program. He was an editor of *Odyssey*, an astronomy and space technology magazine for young people, for eleven years.

Reddy is the author of nine books, including *Halley's Comet, Children's Atlas of the Universe, Children's Atlas of Earth Through Time*, and *Children's Atlas of Native Americans*, plus numerous articles. He was an editor of *Astronomy* magazine for several years.

CONTENTS

Starry Night 5
Our Home: The Milky Way 6
Stages of the Stars 8
Star Groups 11
The Magellanic Clouds 12
The Local Group 15
Galaxies Galore 17
The Spiral Milky Way 18
Great Spiral Beauties 21
Spectacular Ellipticals 22
Black Hole Centers 24
Cannibal Galaxies 27
Fact File: Constellations – Our Map of the
        Milky Way 28

More Books about the Milky Way
        and Other Galaxies 30
Video 30
Places to Visit 30
Places to Write 30
Glossary 31
Index 32

We live in an enormously large place – the Universe. It's just in the last fifty-five years or so that we've found out how large it probably is. It's only natural that we would want to understand the place in which we live, so scientists have developed instruments – such as radio telescopes, satellites, probes, and many more – that have told us far more about the Universe than could possibly be imagined.

We have seen planets up close. We have learned about quasars and pulsars, black holes, and supernovas. We have gathered amazing data about how the Universe may have come into being and how it may end. Nothing could be more astonishing.

Looking toward the sky with unaided eyes, we can see thousands of stars. With telescopes, we can see billions more. Our Sun is just one star in all these billions. Our group of stars is called the Milky Way. We have learned of many other groups of stars, called galaxies, existing in our vast Universe. In this book, you will be given a glimpse of our Galaxy and the billions of galaxies beyond.

Isaac Asimov

Starry Night

After dark, away from city lights, look up at the faint, foggy band encircling the sky. This band is called the Milky Way.

With the invention of the telescope in 1609, early astronomers discovered that the Milky Way is made up of billions of very faint stars.

Astronomers observing the sky in about 1800 saw that the stars exist in a huge collection shaped like a pancake. They named this collection of stars *galaxy*, from the Greek word for "milky way."

Left: This photograph of the Milky Way was taken in the desert of Arizona.

Our Home: The Milky Way

Astronomers first thought our Sun must be located near the center of the Galaxy. But later they found that the center was 24,000 light-years away from our Solar System.

A light-year is the distance traveled by light in one year – nearly 6 trillion miles or 9.5 trillion kilometers. At that speed, light travels from the Sun to Earth in about eight minutes. If you could travel at the speed of light, you could go around the world 7.5 times in just one second!

Our Galaxy is 100,000 light-years across from end to end. It is made up of a central ball of old reddish stars, and a flat outer disk of gas, dust, and young bluish stars. The Milky Way would appear much brighter near its center, but dust clouds hide the center from our view. The Sun is located in the Orion arm of the Galaxy. The Orion, Centaurus, Sagittarius, and Perseus are the four spiral arms of our Galaxy.

Top: Stars are born out of vast clouds of dust and gas located in the arms of our Galaxy. These clouds are called nebulas, or nebulae. Pictured is a nebula in the Sagittarius arm of our Galaxy as seen from an observatory on Earth.

Bottom: The center of the Milky Way. It's not the bright area near the center of the photo. It is the darker, curved band just to the right of the brightness. That is where vast clouds of gas and dust have blotted out our Galaxy's brilliant center.

Opposite: A portrait of the Milky Way Galaxy – notice the four spiral arms swirling out from the center. Our Sun and its family of planets – the Solar System – are in the Milky Way's third arm, which is named for the constellation Orion.

Stages of the Stars

In our Galaxy, there are at least 200 billion stars! Stars form out of large clouds of dust and gas. With so many stars in our Galaxy, there are different kinds of stars at different stages of their lives. Our Sun formed nearly five billion years ago. Other stars are forming today. And since stars don't live forever, many stars are dying at this very moment. The biggest ones eventually explode and add more material to the dust clouds out of which new stars form. Extremely massive stars exist only a few million years before exploding. Our own Sun will live for billions of years before it explodes and forms a red giant star. It will then come to a quiet end as it shrinks into a white dwarf star.

? How did galaxies form? Will we ever know?

Astronomers think that when the Universe formed, it was a small object with all its mass evenly spread out. How did that mass break up into clumps to form the galaxies? Some astronomers think that densely packed matter called black holes formed, dragging in the gas and dust around them with gravitational pull, and then clumping it all together to form stars. That would explain why there are black holes at the centers of galaxies. Other astronomers have other notions, but no one really knows for certain.

Above: The stages in the life of a star like our Sun – At *left* is what is known as an accretion disk, with a glow at its center. It is forming out of a nebula, which is a huge cloud of gas and dust. To its *right* is the star at its longest stage, or what is known as a main sequence star. Our Sun has been at this stage for 4.5 billion years and will stay like this for another 4.5 billion years. Then it will become a red giant *(center)* for about 500 million years, finally shrinking into a white dwarf *(far right)*. The white dwarf will pack most of the Sun's mass into a body about the size of Earth. It will then spend several billion years cooling off.

Left: A supernova *(center)* in the mini-galaxy known as the Large Magellanic Cloud.

Star Groups

The cloud of dust and gas that became our Sun formed only a single star, plus its planets. But such clouds often form more than one star.

Double stars – stars that circle each other – are quite common. Some stars consist of two pairs, even three. In fact, stars begin their lives in large groups, and the sky holds many collections of young stars. There are also globular clusters, which are balls of closely packed stars that may number in the hundreds of thousands. In fact, the entire Galaxy, which is made up of hundreds of billions of stars, probably started as a vast cloud of gas.

Opposite, top: A globular cluster – it is 16,000 light-years from Earth, a close neighbor in globular cluster terms.

Opposite, bottom: From the surface of this imaginary planet, you could see a double-star system *(left)*. These stars rotate around each other. To the *right* is a globular cluster.

Left: The Pleiades star cluster, in the constellation Taurus, formed from an enormous cloud of gas and dust. This cluster is so young that some of the leftover gas from the cloud is still visible.

The Magellanic Clouds

The Milky Way is just one of about 100 billion galaxies in the Universe. For example, in the Southern Hemisphere, two dim clouds can be seen in the night sky that look as though they are pieces of the Milky Way that have broken loose. They are called the Large Magellanic Cloud and the Small Magellanic Cloud. They are named after the explorer Ferdinand Magellan, who was the first European to see them. They are made up of myriads of faint stars. They are known as "irregular" galaxies and are located about 150,000 light-years away. The Large Magellanic Cloud contains about 10 billion stars. The Small Magellanic Cloud holds only about 2 billion stars.

? The mystery of the missing mass

In the past, astronomers thought that most of the mass of any galaxy, up to 90 percent, is located in its center. Astronomers know exactly how the rate of motion should drop off as a star moves farther from the center of a galaxy. When this is actually measured, however, the rate of motion doesn't drop off the way it should. There seems to be more mass in the outer regions than can be seen. So now many scientists think that outer mass could make up 90 percent of galaxies. Perhaps galaxies are surrounded by halos of dim stars or black holes we cannot see. Astronomers call this "the mystery of the missing mass."

Top: People south of the Equator can see the Large Magellanic Cloud without instruments. Astronomers have studied this galaxy to gain insights into our own Galaxy.

Bottom: Also visible to the naked eye south of the Equator is the Small Magellanic Cloud.

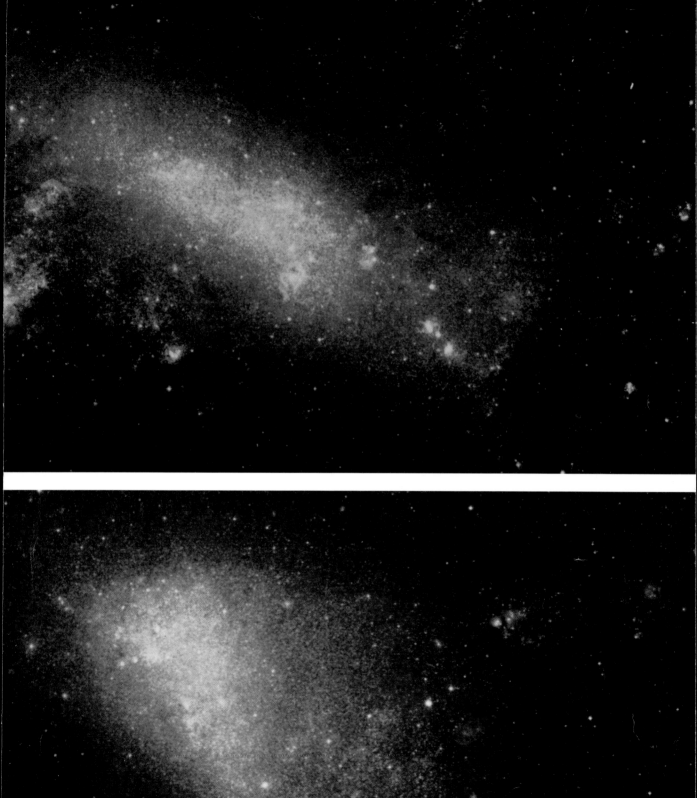

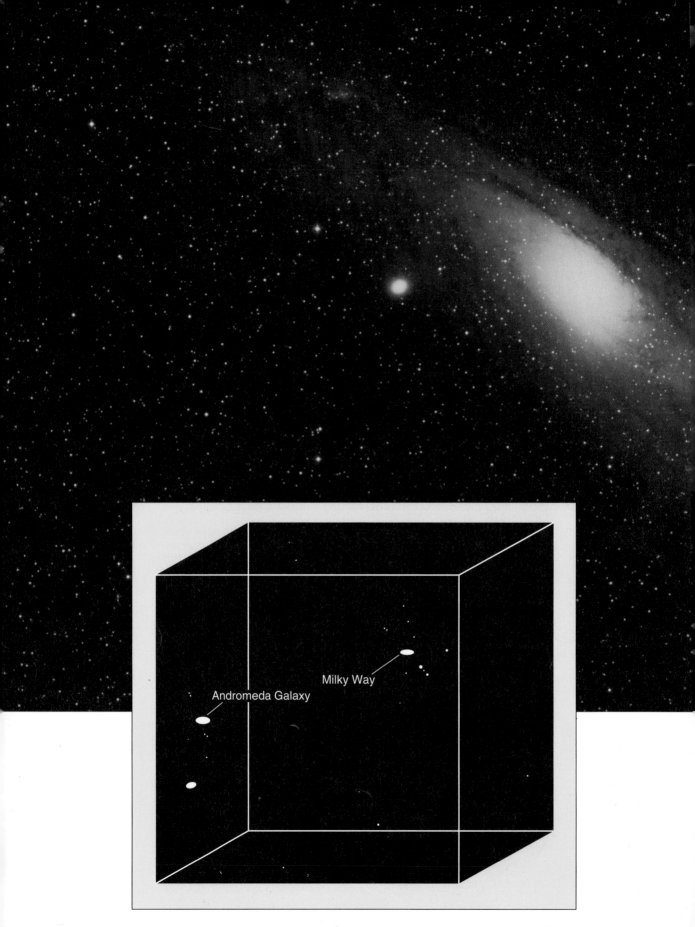

Andromeda Galaxy

Milky Way

The Local Group

In the 1920s, astronomers realized that a faint patch of light in the constellation Andromeda is actually a galaxy far outside our own. It is the Andromeda Galaxy, 2.2 million light-years from the Milky Way.

In addition, there are many other galaxies, much closer to us than the Andromeda Galaxy. These galaxies, the Magellanic Clouds, the Andromeda Galaxy, and the Milky Way make up what is known as the Local Group – all locked together with each other by gravity.

Many members of the Local Group are dwarf galaxies, or galaxies that are just a few times larger than star clusters. One such dwarf galaxy was discovered in 1994. It is so close that one day it might be swallowed up by our Milky Way!

? *Island universes – another name for galaxies?*

In 1755, a German philosopher, Immanuel Kant, wondered about certain foggy patches in the sky. Kant thought these patches were distant collections of stars. He called them "island universes." Other astronomers of the time thought the foggy patches were just clouds of dust and gas fairly close to Earth. It took astronomers nearly two hundred more years to determine that Kant was right about the foggy patches being collections of stars. What Kant called island universes are now called galaxies.

Above: The Andromeda Galaxy, a spiral galaxy like our own Milky Way, is the most distant object that can be seen with the naked eye. It is over two million light-years away. The Andromeda Galaxy is visible in dark country skies during autumn.

Inset: A family portrait of the Local Group. Over the years, astronomers have found several faint, small galaxies – dwarf galaxies – orbiting the Milky Way. The Local Group also contains several so-called irregular galaxies.

Galaxies Galore

A cluster like the Local Group isn't so unusual. Like stars, galaxies usually exist in clusters. Our Local Group is a rather small cluster of galaxies. Other, larger clusters exist, too. In the constellation Coma Berenices, there is a cluster that contains nearly a thousand galaxies. This cluster is about 400 million light-years away. Nearer to us is a cluster of galaxies in the constellation Virgo that is made up of 2,500 galaxies. Recently, a still larger cluster containing over 25,000 galaxies was discovered. Our own Galaxy, huge though it is, is only one of many billions of galaxies in our Universe. We haven't even begun to count them all!

? *Another case of the missing mass?*

Clusters of galaxies are held together by gravity. However, the gravitational pull of the stars in those clusters alone isn't enough to prevent them from drifting apart. That is because there is a lot of mass present that can't be seen. Scientists do not know what is contained in this mass. Very dim stars? Planets? Or mysterious objects never seen before? It may be yet another case of the "missing mass."

Top: A large cluster of galaxies in the constellation Coma Berenices. This cluster contains about a thousand galaxies.

Opposite, bottom, left: The "Siamese Twins" galaxies. They are called this because of the apparent contact between the two galactic disks.

Left: The Virgo cluster of galaxies. This is an irregular cluster, which means that it is not so tightly concentrated toward the cluster's center.

The Spiral Milky Way

Not all galaxies are shaped the same. Many are elliptical, or oval-shaped. Others are spirals, with flat, round, swirly shapes.

Our Milky Way is a spiral galaxy. Its outer regions are made up of long, curved lines of stars, called spiral arms. These curve into the central part of the Galaxy. Astronomers trace the spiral arms by following the young, giant blue stars they contain.

The Orion arm contains our Sun. It is the third of the Milky Way's four arms. The Centaurus and Sagittarius arms are closer to the center of the Galaxy, and the Perseus arm is farthest from the center. All the stars in these arms move around the center of the Galaxy. The Sun circles the center once every 230 million years.

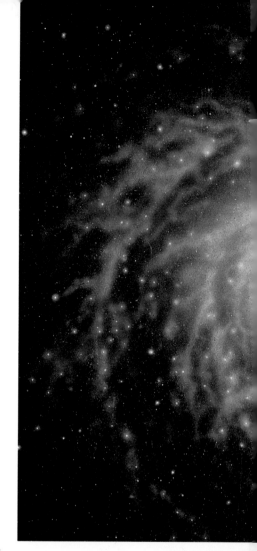

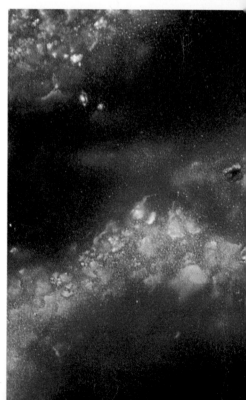

Top: Two views of the Milky Way Galaxy – at *left* is a face-on view, with the spirals whirling around the center; at *right* is a view from the side, with the spirals forming a disk intersected by the center. The center bulges with old stars, while the spiral arms are the home of brightly shining new stars.

Opposite, bottom, right: Here is a closer look at the images above, with some of the major parts of our Galaxy pointed out.

Right: Because our Solar System is on the inner edge of the Orion arm, we get a spectacular view of the next innermost arm – the Sagittarius arm, pictured.

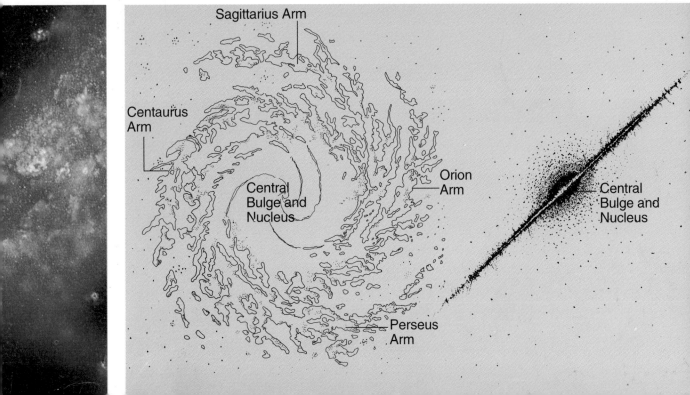

Sagittarius Arm

Centaurus
Arm

Central
Bulge and
Nucleus

Orion
Arm

Central
Bulge and
Nucleus

Perseus
Arm

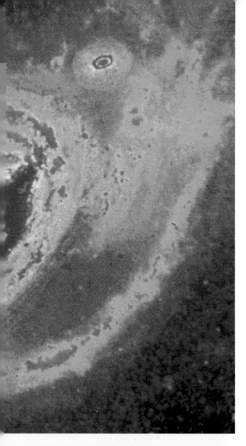

Great Spiral Beauties

Our Milky Way is a wonderful sight. But, of course, we can only see it from the inside, so we don't get a good overall view of it. However, we can see other galaxies, and some of them have beautiful spiral shapes, especially if we happen to see them face-on. The Whirlpool Galaxy is perhaps the most beautiful of the spirals. The spiral Andromeda Galaxy is at a slant, but the arms can still be seen. Only the edges of some spiral galaxies, like the Sombrero Galaxy, are visible. With these spirals, a line of dust clouds can usually be seen along the edge of the rim. Almost every spiral galaxy is beautiful in its own way.

Opposite, top, left: The M81 Galaxy is one of the most visible and familiar of the spiral galaxies. The computer-enhanced picture shows the younger stars that make up the arms as blue and the older stars of the disk as orange.

Opposite, bottom: Do you see why this spiral galaxy is called the Sombrero Galaxy?

Left: A spiral galaxy visible from Earth's Southern Hemisphere.

Top, right: A false-color picture of a spiral galaxy with a possible black hole at its center.

Center: Dust clouds across the plane of a spiral galaxy blot out the light of background stars. The next time you go barefoot in your yard or in a park, think about how every particle of soil under your feet once floated in space in clouds like these.

Spectacular Ellipticals

Many galaxies do not have spiral structures. They seem to be made up just of centers, without arms. These galaxies are called elliptical galaxies because their outlines are oval. Most elliptical galaxies are rather dim – but they can be giants.

Large clusters of galaxies are often made up of ellipticals, and the largest contain up to a hundred times as many stars as our Galaxy contains!

❓ *How many stars did you say?*

The average galaxy may have about 100,000,000,000 (a hundred billion) stars. Some giant elliptical galaxies have a hundred times that number. On the other hand, there are many dwarf galaxies with only one-tenth the average number.

Still, if a hundred billion stars per galaxy is the average and if there are about a hundred billion galaxies, the total number of stars in the Universe is about ten sextillion. That's 10,000,000,000,000,000,000, 000 stars!

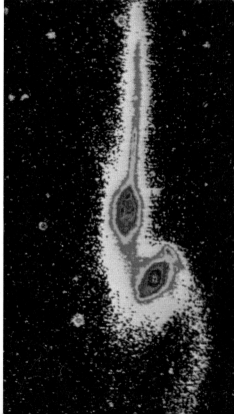

Top: Centaurus A is one of the brightest and largest of the known galaxies. Scientists believe that giant explosions involving millions of stars are occurring at this galaxy's center. The matter ejected by these explosions appears as the dark band across the galactic disk.

Opposite, bottom: Pictured is a variety of galaxy types as seen from an imaginary planet. Can you tell the ellipticals from the spirals?

Right: Some galaxies interact and even collide with each other. This computer-enhanced picture shows streams of gas created by the interaction of two so-called "mouse" galaxies.

Black Hole Centers

The powerful activity at the centers of galaxies requires a lot of energy. Astronomers have long suspected that the energy comes from the gravity of colossal black holes located there.

In 1994, astronomers using the Hubble Space Telescope proved that at least one galaxy, M-87, has a giant black hole at its center. The black hole would account for the mysterious jet of matter shooting out from the center of the galaxy.

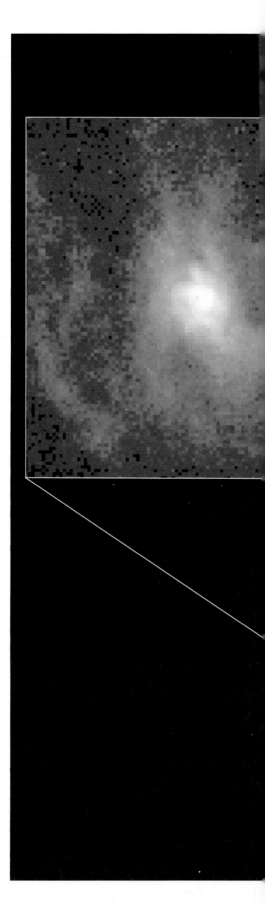

❗ *Very – make that incredibly – distant galaxies*

There are galaxies that are very far – over a billion light-years – away. A few galaxies that are that far away have very active centers. Those centers blaze so brightly they can be seen even when the rest of the galaxy cannot be. At one time, astronomers detected certain dim stars they thought belonged to our own Galaxy. Imagine their surprise when they realized they were looking at the centers of incredibly distant galaxies. Those far-off active centers were named quasars. They are among the most distant objects in the Universe!

Right: The M-87 Galaxy is the home of the very first known black hole. The Hubble Space Telescope peered into the heart of the galaxy to see a swirling disk that created the jet that is visible in the *upper right*. The disk itself is shown in the inset at *upper left*.

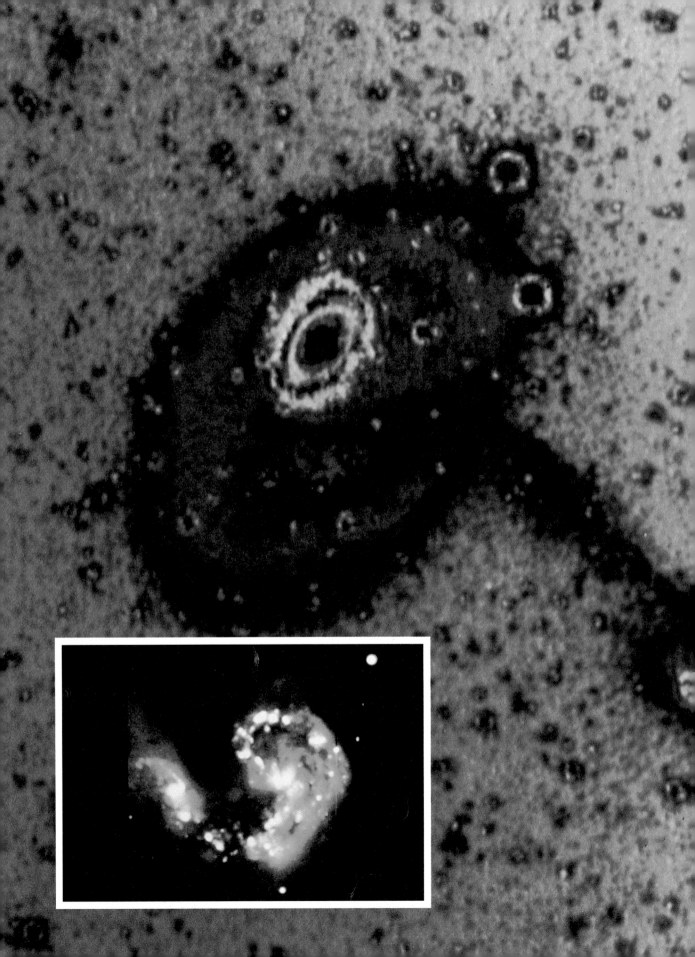

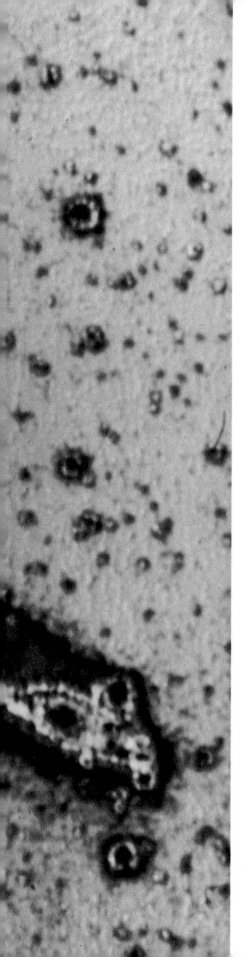

Cannibal Galaxies

It's a big Universe. In most cases, stars are so far apart that they pass each other harmlessly. But galaxies in clusters do move around. As a result, some galaxies collide with each other.

Colliding galaxies can have an effect on one another. The breaking up of dust clouds, for example, can produce a lot of radiation. And if galaxies collide head on, they sometimes remain together. In fact, the giant galaxies in some clusters may be as large as they are because they have swallowed others. The giants are sometimes called "cannibal galaxies" for that reason.

We cannot be sure, but in four billion years or so, our Galaxy may collide with the Andromeda Galaxy. Who knows what the effects would be? For now, at least, we're safe in our corner of the Milky Way!

Left: A computer-enhanced picture of two so-called "toadstool" galaxies in collision. These galaxies are connected by a bridge of gas. The bridge is lit by bright, young stars.

Inset: A dramatic collision between two galaxies forms a pair of "antennae" or "rattail" galaxies, 90 million light-years from Earth. This encounter began 500 million years ago.

Fact File: Constellations –
Our Map of the Milky Way

When you look into the sky at the Milky Way, you see stars – thousands of them at once. Some of these stars stand out from the rest. For centuries, people have believed that certain stars form patterns or even pictures in the sky.

These patterns of stars are called constellations. Most constellations are named after gods and heroes from ancient Greek mythology, animals, scientific instruments, and various objects that were in common use long ago.

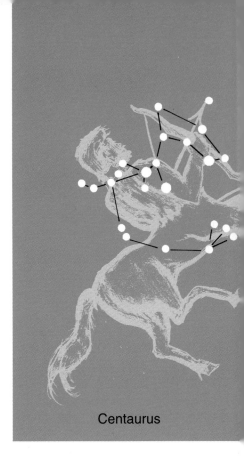

Centaurus

The stars that make up any one constellation are not actually close together. They just look that way from our viewpoint.

Constellations help us find stars, planets, and other objects in the sky. They are our map of the Milky Way.

The Galaxy of Numbers

How big and far away are objects in the Universe? You probably know what a 2-story school building looks like. If you have ever watched a baseball game, you can imagine 90 feet (27.5 meters) – the distance between each base. And you can probably figure out about how long 2 hours seems – or 24 hours, which makes 1 day.

But what if we say that light travels nearly 6 trillion miles (9.5 trillion km) in a year? That's quite another story. And what if, to make matters worse, we say that the Milky Way Galaxy is 100,000 light-years across?

This would mean that the Milky Way is 100,000 times 6 trillion miles (9.5 trillion km) across! Can you imagine numbers that large?

Reading about galaxies means reading about time and space – usually huge amounts of time and space. It means numbers so large that it may be impossible to understand exactly what they mean. We can never understand from anything we do in our day-to-day lives.

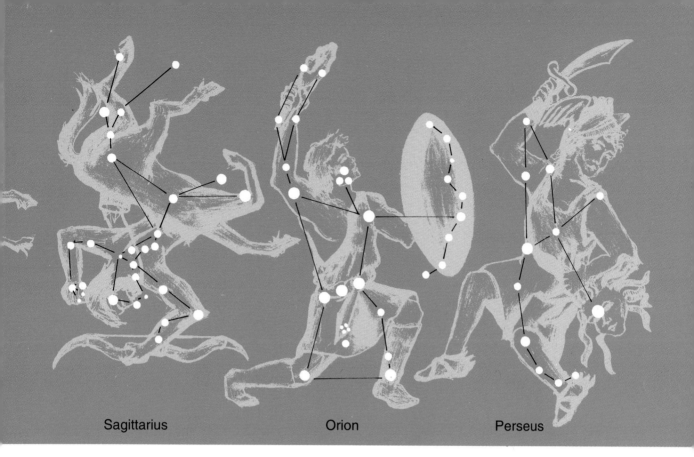

Sagittarius   Orion   Perseus

Above: The spiral arms of our Galaxy have been named after these four constellations. *Left to right*, they are Centaurus, the Centaur, half man and half horse; Sagittarius, the Archer; Orion, the Hunter; and Perseus, the hero who killed Medusa, the creature that turned people to stone.

But perhaps we can imagine, if we start with numbers that are small –

- The 18 sheets of paper that make up this book total just over 1/16 inch (about 2 millimeters) in thickness.

- A **million** sheets of paper would be as high as a 32-story building.

- A **billion** sheets of paper would be over 55 miles (90 km) tall – 10 times taller than Mt. Everest!

- A **trillion** sheets would tower more than 59,000 miles (95,000 km) above Earth – more than one-quarter of the way to the Moon!

- If we figure 60 seconds to a minute, and 60 minutes to an hour, then 86,400 seconds make up a 24-hour day.

- A **million** seconds is 12 days.

- A **billion** seconds is more than 31 years.

- A **trillion** seconds adds up to 300 centuries. That's 30,000 years. Thirty thousand years ago, many of our ancestors were still living in caves!

No matter how you look at it, one thing is certain: The numbers may be small to begin with, but jumping from a million to a billion to a trillion is no small matter. How quickly small numbers become astronomical!

More Books about the Milky Way and Other Galaxies

The Birth of Our Universe. Asimov (Gareth Stevens)
Once Around the Galaxy. Gallant (Franklin Watts)
Planets and Galaxies. Mackie (Penworthy)
Space Tour. Mackie (Hayes)
Stars and Galaxies. Apfel (Franklin Watts)

Video

Our Milky Way and Other Galaxies. (Gareth Stevens)

Places to Visit

You can explore our Milky Way and other galaxies in the Universe without leaving Earth.
Here are some museums and centers where you can find a variety of space exhibits.

NASA Lyndon B. Johnson Space Center
2101 NASA Road One
Houston, TX 77058

Edmonton Space and Science Centre
11211 - 142nd Street
Edmonton, Alberta T5M 4A1

National Air and Space Museum
Smithsonian Institution
Seventh and Independence Avenue SW
Washington, D.C. 20560

Australian Museum
6-8 College Street
Sydney, NSW 2000 Australia

San Diego Aero-Space Museum
2001 Pan American Plaza - Balboa Park
San Diego, CA 92101

The Space and Rocket Center
  and Space Camp
One Tranquility Base
Huntsville, AL 35807

Places to Write

Here are some places you can write for more information about our Milky Way and other galaxies.
Be sure to state what kind of information you would like. Include your full name and address so
they can write back to you.

National Space Society
922 Pennsylvania Avenue SE
Washington, D.C. 20003

National Museum of Science
  and Technology
P. O. Box 9724
Station T
Ottawa, Ontario K1G 5A3

The Planetary Society
65 North Catalina
Pasadena, CA 91106

Sydney Observatory
P. O. Box K346
Haymarket 2000 Australia

Glossary

accretion disk: a ring of interstellar matter surrounding a star or other object, such as a black hole.

astronomers: people who study the various bodies of the Universe.

billion: the number represented by 1 followed by nine zeroes – 1,000,000,000. In some countries, this number is called "a thousand million." In these countries, one billion would then be represented by 1 followed by twelve zeroes – 1,000,000,000,000 – a million million.

black hole: a massive object – usually a collapsed star – so tightly packed that not even light can escape the force of its gravity.

cannibal galaxies: giant galaxies that have collided with and "swallowed" other galaxies.

constellation: a grouping of stars in the sky that seems to trace out a familiar figure or symbol.

double stars: stars that circle each other.

elliptical: shaped like an oval.

galaxy: any of the billions of large groupings of stars, gas, and dust that exist in the Universe. Our Galaxy is known as the Milky Way.

globular star clusters: ball-shaped groupings of closely packed stars. These clusters are smaller than galaxies, although there may be hundreds of thousands of stars in each ball.

light-year: the distance that light travels in one year – nearly 6 trillion miles (9.5 trillion km).

Milky Way: the name of our Galaxy. From Earth's position in the Galaxy, the Milky Way looks like a river of stars in the night sky.

Orion arm: that part of our Milky Way Galaxy where our Sun is located.

spiral arms: long, curved lines of stars. Our Milky Way consists of such spiral arms.

Sun: our star and provider of the energy that makes life possible on Earth.

Universe: everything that we know exists and that we believe may exist.

Index

accretion disk 8-9
Andromeda Galaxy 14-15, 21, 27
antennae galaxies 26-27

black holes 8, 20-21, 24-25

cannibal galaxies 27
Centaurus 6, 18, 29
Centaurus A 22-23
colliding galaxies 26-27
Coma Berenices 16-17
constellations 6, 11, 15, 17, 28-29

double stars 10-11
dwarf galaxies 14-15, 22

elliptical galaxies 18, 22-23
Equator 12-13

globular clusters 10-11
Greek mythology 28-29

Hubble Space Telescope 24-25

irregular galaxies 12-17
island universes 15

Kant, Immanuel 15

Large Magellanic Cloud 8-9, 12-13
light-years 6, 10-11, 12, 14-15, 17, 24-25, 26-27, 28
Local Group 14-15, 17

M87 Galaxy 24-25
Magellan, Ferdinand 12
Magellanic Clouds 8-9, 12-13, 15

main sequence stars 9
Milky Way 4-5, 6-7, 12, 14-15, 18-19, 21, 27, 28
missing mass 12, 17
mouse galaxies 22

nebulae 6, 8-9

Orion 6-7, 18-19, 29

Perseus 6, 18-19, 29
Pleiades 10-11

quasars 24

radiation 27
rattail galaxies 26-27
red giants 9

Sagittarius 6, 18-19, 29
Siamese Twins galaxies 16-17
Small Magellanic Cloud 12-13
Solar System 6-7, 18-19
Sombrero Galaxy 20-21
Southern Hemisphere 12, 21
spiral galaxies 14-15, 18-19, 20-21, 22
Sun 6-7, 8-9, 11, 18
supernovas 8-9

Taurus 10-11
telescopes 5
toadstool galaxies 26-27

Virgo 16-17

Whirlpool Galaxy 21
white dwarfs 8-9

Born in 1920, Isaac Asimov came to the United States as a young boy from his native Russia. As a young man, he was a student of biochemistry. In time, he became one of the most productive writers the world has ever known. His books cover a spectrum of topics, including science, history, language theory, fantasy, and science fiction. His brilliant imagination gained him the respect and admiration of adults and children alike. Sadly, Isaac Asimov died shortly after the publication of the first edition of *Isaac Asimov's Library of the Universe*.

The publishers wish to thank the following for permission to reproduce copyright material: front cover, © Garret Moore; 4-5, © Frank Zullo 1985; 6 (upper), Anglo-Australian Telescope Board, David Malin; 6 (lower), © Frank Zullo 1987; 7, 8-9 (upper), © Julian Baum 1988; 8-9 (lower), National Optical Astronomy Observatories; 10, © Julian Baum 1988; 10-11 (upper), National Optical Astronomy Observatories; 10-11 (lower), © John Foster; 12-13 (both), © ROE/Anglo-Australian Observatory, David Malin; 14, © Gareth Stevens Inc.; 14-15, NASA; 16, 16-17 (both), National Optical Astronomy Observatories; 18-19 (upper), © Lynette Cook 1987; 18-19 (lower), © Sally Bensusen 1987; 19, Sheri Gibbs; 20 (upper left), Halton C. Arp; 20 (upper right), Official US Naval Photograph, US Naval Observatory; 20 (lower), National Optical Astronomy Observatories; 20-21, Halton C. Arp; 21, Anglo-Australian Telescope Board, David Malin; 22, 22-23, National Optical Astronomy Observatories; 23, © Garret Moore; 24-25, Holland Ford/NASA; 26, 26-27, National Optical Astronomy Observatories; 28-29, © Laurie Shock 1988.